This book is not meant to replace guidance or help from professionals in this subject. The authors are merely sharing what they have learned, their journey, and offering friendly direction. The authors recommend seeking professional help for those with deeper issues.

For permissions, write: Soft Touch Publishing | Subject Line: Good Grief | softtouchpublishing@outlook.com

Editors: Angela K. Durden and Tom Whitfield

GOOD GRIEF
VALERIE D. SWINTON
FRED J. KIRBY

SOFT TOUCH PUBLISHING
SNELLVILLE, GEORGIA

This book is dedicated to God,
who gave us the vision.

To all the families around the world that have lost loved ones, we dedicate this book to you. Just know you are loved, needed, and you will get through your grief in due time.

We also dedicate this book to our beloved spouses Carolyn Kirby and John J. Swinton for their unselfish love encouraging us to continue moving forward with our lives.

GOOD
GRIEF
A JOURNEY FROM LOST TO LOVE
Valerie D. Swinton
Fred J. Kirby, Jr.
GUIDED GRIEF JOURNEY INCLUDED

"And He will wipe out every tear from their eyes, and death will be no more, neither will mourning nor outcry nor pain be anymore. The former things have passed away."

Revelation 21:4

Introduction

Until it is swallowed up forever at God's command (Isaiah 25:8), the sting of death is harsh, often brutal, for those left behind.

While divorce, moving, major illness/injury, and job loss round out the list of the top five most stressful life events, leading the list is the death of a loved one. We, the authors of this book, each lost lovely, wonderful spouses to long illnesses after lengthy marriages. One thing our spouses had in common was this: They encouraged us to continue living and to find another mate. In fact, they insisted we not put our hearts and lives on a shelf.

At the time, of course, we couldn't imagine doing that. But our spouses were wise and, though it wasn't easy, we did as they asked. Of course, the big question was would either of us find another such wonderful person to again be in our lives. We dated others, but they were not keepers; mind you, not because they weren't good people, we simply were not a fit.

And then one day we found each other. More on that later. Right now, we would like you to know why we are writing this book. It is to share some important things we've learned as we moved on after our spouses passed away. We gained a deeper awareness of grace, and even in tragedy grace helped us to discover our purpose and rediscover who we are individually. Still on our journey, we want people to understand and know that you are:

- stronger than you think
- needed
- loved
- going to get through it
- going to make a difference
- alive for a reason

New circumstances require adjustments, continued growth, and constant struggle, but strong faith in God conquers all. We have always had faith.

However, our faith became stronger as we discovered other ideas and perspectives, including spiritual ones, and developed a closer personal relationship with God.

So, here you are.

Still among the living. Have you felt guilty that you are still alive? Like grit in a shoe makes a journey longer and more miserable, survivor's guilt wears down a heart and soul. It takes a toll on energy levels.

Survivor's guilt is a negative emotion and rarely produces anything good.

You will go through your journey at your pace. There is no right or wrong timing for grieving — or moving forward. Even our Heavenly Father tells us there is a time to be still and wait. (Ruth 3:18; 2 Chronicles 20:17)

Don't rush through the grieving process. Everyone grieves in the way that is best for them. There are no rules for how that process happens, what grief looks like, the order one goes through the stages of grief — denial, anger, bargaining, depression, acceptance — or the duration of any part of it. Despite what you go through, don't give up on life. In Ecclesiastes

11:6, King Solomon commented upon the benefits of moving forward when he said, "In the morning sow your seed and until the evening do not let your hand rest; for you are not knowing where this will have success, either here or there or whether both of them will alike to good."

There is hope in new beginnings. You can have a fine future, and even redefine or strengthen your purpose in life after a loved one passes. As you work toward healing, all this will come with time.

You are not the only one going through changes. As you begin to reengage with the world through dating, children, relatives, even some friends may not accept the new person, and could get jealous and angry with you and them, feeling you have betrayed their friend, mother, or father. Often heard from even grown children is "He's not my Dad!" or "She's not my mother!"

Your timing and their timing may not match up. The only one that matters is yours.

If you have lost a loved one to death and are wondering how, when, or even if, you should move forward, then this book just might help you. Marriage is "until death do us part". God puts us in people's lives for a season – and a reason. You may very well still have a purpose to fulfill on this earth. You owe it to yourself – and your loved ones still living on this earth – to explore that possibility. Open yourself up to God's communications with you.

If you are trying to find your purpose in life, (i.e. love, companionship, friendship, relationship with God, family, etc.), then by all means allow this book to present positive information and differing viewpoints for your mind, heart, soul, and spirit to feed upon. Dark days do not need to remain thus. After experiencing a loss of a loved one, know that your life can be transformed to something beautiful.

To live in hearts we leave behind is not to die.

Thomas Campbell

PART ONE

The importance of God in your journey through grief

We write this book toward Christians – that is, those who profess belief in Almighty God and His Son and His word the Bible. However, we are also aware some may have found this book who are without a belief in God or with belief in an unnamed and undefined higher power, with no particular doctrine, or who have not read the Bible. It is not our intent to go into doctrinal matters per se. Our focus is purely the death of a spouse and how to move on.

Therefore, any cited scriptures here have proven to be good advice for anyone, anywhere, over millennia. Shakespeare was a great one for quoting Scripture yet taking all the credit for the brilliant turns of phrases that were by the writers of Psalms, Proverbs, Ecclesiastes, and other Bible books.

We are saying all this for two reasons. One: If you are a non-Christian, don't be put off by the scripture citations or the mention of our Heavenly Father, the underlying basic advice will still be good because the journey through the tragedy of losing a beloved mate is a common human experience.

And two: Losing your mate may be causing you to have thoughts and feelings you've never had before. You might very well be having a hard time naming those feelings or even understanding those thoughts. To that we say this: You may be coming into contact with your spiritual core, a core you may not have known you have. This is not an uncommon occurrence and this book could serve as a gentle guide through that.

Sometimes we may feel, as did the psalmist (Psalms 119:176), as if we are wandering like a lost sheep and have been forgotten by our Heavenly Father. Does He see us? Does He care? Jesus said God knows the number of hairs on our head (Matthew 10:30), so you can rest assured He knows our grief.

Our Heavenly Father transcends time. Psalms 90:4 says, "For a thousand years are in your eyes but as yesterday when it is past..." This tells us His patience is long. It is not He who is pushing us to "get over" our grief. Anyone who says otherwise is incorrect and not being helpful.

Ecclesiastes 3:1-8 says there is a time for being born and a time to die. A time to break down and a time to build up. A time to weep and a time to laugh…and more.

So, just what is the role of God in your journey through grief? What part does He play? What does He want for you…and from you? And how can you know and find it? Let us, Fred and Valerie, share a bit of our stories.

Fred shares:

God played an important role in my life from early on. I was the fourth child out of six sons or, as I would say it, "the oldest of the youngest three". Grandfather was a farmer who lived "just a yell away". I grew up on a farm with God-fearing parents; we were at church almost every Sunday. And yes, I did my share of working on the farm. Hard labor prepared me for my purpose.

A year after high school I joined the United States Air Force, where I was further groomed and challenged. After that, I moved to Atlanta where I met my wife, Carolyn. We were married just shy of 20 years during which, by the grace of God, we had a child.

I say "by the grace of God" because early in her pregnancy Carolyn was diagnosed with an autoimmune disease, scleroderma, causing the pregnancy to be high-risk. She went into remission, though. God gave her more time to prepare our son and me for life without her.

1 Corinthians 10:13 says that God "will not let you be tempted beyond what you can bear" and will "make a way out in order for you to be able to endure it". James 1:2-4 says that we should consider it all joy when we meet with various trials because this "tested quality of your faith works out endurance" so that it can produce a complete and sound person, not lacking in anything.

What God wanted for me after my wife's long illnesses (scleroderma and Raynaud's) and her death was to be happy, be strong, and be faithful. Without Him, there is no journey. He simply wanted me to trust and believe in Him...not that it has been easy, but the tested quality of my faith has allowed me to endure certain trials.

First, my wife's death. Then my son fathering a child with his girlfriend and he wasn't even out of high school yet.

How could I deal with a grandchild without my beloved helpmeet?

Carolyn truly wanted me to be happy, too. She encouraged me to have a good life and enjoy it after she was gone. And so, after she passed, I dated. All of the women were good people. Each was different and I liked each differently. One I even dated for nine years; even considered marriage. Each of those women were in my life for a reason and a season. I asked myself why I was "dating" for so long? Was it because I was going along to get along? Was I helping someone else fulfill their dream? And, most importantly, I had to ask myself two very big questions: Was God happy with me simply "settling"?

Also, would Carolyn approve?

But you know what? Each had a part in leading me to where I needed to be. And that was when I met Valerie D. Swinton, my coauthor of this book. We have so much in common. We traveled parallel paths almost at the same time, each dealing with sick spouses.

We crossed paths at God's speed.

Valerie shares:

After being married 24 years to John, my high school sweetheart and love of my life, holding multiple demanding roles of wife and mother and all that implies, then add to that the stress of being a caregiver, as well as donating a kidney to him, you can well imagine how spread thin I was. Even if the role of long-term caregiver had not been part of the mix, losing a mate and having my child become independent changed the frame of my daily schedule. I was not ready for him to leave this earth.

Now I had no one to direct the order of my days. I was on my own. If I'm no longer a wife and caregiver, then who am I? As I discovered — and rebuilt — my personality and motivation, I found shortcomings that needed addressing. Thank God I did not have to address these on my own. God led me through an examination that allowed me to see not only who I was but who I needed to be.

Part of that involved developing a more intimate relationship with my Heavenly Father. As with all relationships, the one with our Father in heaven will change. There is an ebb and flow, an up and down, with that bond. *This is normal.*

There are many who believe that our relationship with God must remain at a fever pitch at all times or else we've lost all faith and we are no longer worthy of His love. *That is simply not true.*

From the prophets to the psalmists and the apostles to the early Christians, not a one of them was perfect. Not a one did all things right all the time. They got tired and discouraged and made harmful decisions and felt as if there was no hope for that which afflicted them at the time. But all did the same sorts of things to get through their difficult times.

One: They spent quiet time reviewing what they knew to be the truth of their Heavenly

Father's dealings with His people and comparing that to their personal expectations or how they believe He's dealt with them.

Two: They recognized the lies Satan wanted them to believe (one being they were not worthy of God's love and attention!) and rejected those lies, thus taking away His enemy's power.

Three: They read, studied, and contemplated deeply His words found in the Holy Bible.

Four: They engaged in consistent prayers of thanks and supplication.

Fred and I were both doing that before we met each other, and have continued to do so. Even as we work on this book, we are finding more opportunities for refinement. Sure, it isn't easy and, to quote a famous cliché, nothing worthwhile ever is.

Our Father knows no two people are the same and He knows we will go through our journey in our way. But we don't always know that, so we have well-meaning friends, pastors, relatives, and total strangers offer us a list of do's and don'ts that they promise will solve whatever ails us. So, we do those things but we may get even more depressed because those things aren't working. Who do we blame for that lack of success?

Ourselves!

The truth of the matter, though, is that rules only work in limited situations, whereas principles work in a huge number of circumstances, conditions, and settings. Principles are flexible, rules are not. Therefore, as we offer our individual stories, we are simply showing you how God-focused **principles** worked for us as we were on our path. Therefore, one thing Fred and I do not want to do in this book is to give hard and fast "rules" for this journey.

PART TWO
What is grief?

When we lose someone we love we learn not to live with them, but to live with the love they left behind.

Anonymous

In most versions or translations of the Bible, there are over 50 scriptures that specifically mention the words grief, grief-stricken, grieved, and grieving. Grief from bereavement involves emotional suffering. That emotion, if not acknowledged, can cause illness in the body.

Grief can also produce changes in a person's personality. For instance, a normally calm person could become agitated, even uncharacteristically angry.

An outgoing person could withdraw, isolating themselves, maybe because they cannot handle any more reminders of their loss when friends hug them.

They may feel hopeless, abandoned by God.

They may ignore health matters, eat too much or not enough, not bathe or change their clothes often.

Ability to remember or concentrate may affect job and other responsibilities such as paying bills. Even restful sleep may be lost as Psalm 119:28 says, "My soul has been sleepless from grief."

These are normal responses and nothing to unduly worry about. Certainly, nothing over which to beat yourself up.

We both knew our spouses were facing death and therefore, some might say, we had time to plan ahead for that, maybe even grieve with our spouses. Still, after their deaths grief came in all its influence, in its own time, and in its own way.

Valerie:

My journey with God started when I was very young. Both of my parents were very active in the church and community we lived in. Their seven children were also active, attending church services on a regular basis on Sundays with our family. My parents were very adamant about that.

At the age of 9 I received my first Bible in 1967 from my pastor after completing several classes at church. I still have that Bible. I also attended Bible study and Vacation Bible School, sang in the youth choir, participated in church plays, and assisted in the church nursery. When I became a teenager, I was asked to teach one of the elementary Sunday School classes.

In addition to all those things, I was an Acolyte whose duties were to light the candles during service. I was involved in the Youth Ministry where we traveled to convalescent homes to comfort the elderly with songs, and we went caroling at Christmas throughout our neighborhood. A lot of these activities continued throughout college.

There have been four people in my life very dear to my heart but whose loss caused me to encounter grief.

The first time I met grief was when Mother passed away. I was 10. I didn't know how to feel. I knew I was sad and missed Mother terribly, but as I stared at her casket I thought, "Who's going to take care of me and my six siblings, cook our meals, do my hair?" At her funeral, sitting in the pew with family, I felt lost and unsure about my future. Several adults said Mother was looking down at me from the sky and smiling. So what would you expect a little girl to do? Why, go outside and look up to the sky, of course. But all I saw was cloudy sky, not Mother smiling at me. I was confused and didn't understand what I was feeling was grief.

Eight years later came my second encounter with grief. My youngest brother died in an accident. I was devastated. Although the accident wasn't my fault, I felt hurt and guilty — I was a busy 18-year-old packing to go to college — because I was the last to lay eyes on him. Oh, how I wish I would have stopped him from going boating!

Along with my mother and brother's deaths, I lost grandparents and other family members, but the grieving process was different because I didn't have a close relationship with them since they lived far away in other states.

Then when I was 25, living on my own in another state from where I grew up, I received a call from one of my older siblings. Father had passed away from a massive heart attack. He was the only parent I had left!

He'd been with me all of my life. I still depended on him. And thus grief was, yet again, met face to face.

Then twenty-one years went by during which my husband had been on dialysis with Chronic Kidney Disease, also called CKD. After the birth of our only child, we found out that we had the same blood type and I was able to donate one of my kidneys in 2004, giving him nine more years of life.

Before my husband passed away, we had a conversation. Should he die before me, John said he wanted me to keep living. If I wanted to date or get married, do it. John gave me his blessings to find love again. He was not selfish. He was unwavering: He didn't want me to crawl up in a ball and feel sorry for myself, but to continue living my life to the fullest until it was my time to be with the Lord.

We did not know we had the same blood type until our son was born. We waited until our child was older to do the transplant. It was amazing that we were a perfect match; that was nothing but God's grace. During twenty-four years of marriage I saw my husband's health deteriorate. He was a man of very strong faith. But he never complained as he went in and out of the hospital, or when he took dialysis three times a week yet still went to work every day and — this was amazing — continued his roles as father and husband. He completed two degrees, Bachelor of Science in Computer Information Systems (1987), and while going through the transplant completed his Master of Business Administration (2004).

John loved me dearly and Collin, his son, was his heart. He did everything the Lord wanted him to do on this earth until he went to be with the Lord. It was all in God's plan.

He was phenomenal. My husband died on January 7, 2013, from a massive heart attack. After years and years of dialysis, his heart simply gave out.

God will let His children go through things yet at the time we may not know why. Going through the journeys of losing my loved ones enabled me to prepare to handle the death of my husband.

But, grieving for him did not began until after his funeral. I was so involved in planning that my mind was very occupied. He passed away on a Monday and we had the funeral Saturday of that week. I felt like I was moving a mile a minute as well as floating in space and in a trance all at the same time. I was just going through the motions.

Also, during this time, I was very much concerned with my son, Collin. You see, it was his last semester of his senior year in high school and he and his father were very close. I was more concerned with how Collin was doing and feeling than with my own grief. I was trying hard to be strong for him.

I will never forget my son saying, "Dad lasted on this earth until I was 18 years old. He taught me how to be a man."

But after family and friends had gone home and went back to their normal routines, I felt a sense of darkness come upon me. Everything happened so fast. I was angry, felt alone, and was disappointed with God that he took my loving, kind, and sweet husband away from me and my son. I didn't want to be around a lot of people, just wanted to take in everything that had transpired. Now, I had to be the mother and father for my son and deal with everything that was ahead of me. In my heart, I knew God loved me and that He was with me, but still…it was hard. John was a great provider for his family, a loving husband, and a fine father.

I remember opening a drawer where he kept his hair brush and smelling it, as well as going into his closet to breathe in his scent. I'd then drop to my knees, bawling my eyes out like a baby, screaming, and asking God *Why?*

I was scared and afraid of the unknown future of my life and son. Then one night while I was sleeping, I opened my eyes to see my husband standing at the side of our bed, looking over me. He told me everything was going to be alright and our son and I would be just fine, and that he loved us very much.

Then he disappeared.

I threw back the covers, sat up, and said, "I must be dreaming."

Another time soon after his passing, I was driving home and started thinking about how much he was missed. Again, I was crying so uncontrollably I had to stop on the side of the road. The Holy Spirit spoke to me: "I will never leave you. I am with you always."

During my grieving process, both my son and I went to counseling a couple of times. It was somewhat helpful. The grief counselor said that the first year after a death is the most difficult because as you go into the holidays, a birthday, anniversary, etc., it will be lonely without your loved one.

Yes, it was difficult. But as the years went on the grief became…I don't want to say easier, that would be misleading…so I'll say I was more comfortable with my reaction to it.

Because his father passed at the beginning of our son's second semester of his senior high school year, I now went alone to his basketball games, graduation, other memorable occasions, and assisted as he visited colleges and universities. Of course, family came to graduations and some games, but it wasn't the same without John being there.

One great thing was that my husband had an opportunity to see our son's high school senior pictures. He was also able to celebrate our son's eighteenth birthday, attended sports-related activities, and was really excited when our son received several college acceptance letters. We also were able to celebrate Thanksgiving, Christmas, and New Year's once more before his death.

Some people never want to change a thing when their loved one dies. They keep the house the same, leave clothes in closets, keep all pictures on the walls just as before. Others make a lot of changes as to decorations and pictures.

I changed my bedroom.

Then I went through the house and made other changes. I allowed only a few family pictures of me, my son, and husband together to remain visible because my son was still living at home.

Some things helped me with the grieving process and kept me moving along. After my son went to college, I got a part-time job. I also went on some tour group trips abroad as well as other local trips just to get away from the house. I joined Facebook groups for widows (such as Widows In Stilettos). I did activities with others to give and get support. A few years later my granddaughter was born. There is nothing like a new life coming into the world to help you deal with grief. She has occupied a lot of my time, and happily so.

Other things that helped me through my grieving process were attending faith conferences, listening to faith leaders on television, my church family, and my pastor. I also found writing about this journey helped tremendously to navigate the path I was walking. [See the Guided Grief Journey at the back of the book on page 103.]

I used to visit my husband's grave on a regular basis. Some people would think this was strange but I'd talk to John and update him on what was going on in my life. I kept him informed of Collin's life and, in general, things going on. I saved some of his workout shirts and his workout gloves that I still use to this day. These all brought comfort to my heart.

Now I only go to place flowers at his grave on holidays, Father's Day, and his birthday. I remember him telling me once that he didn't want me to do that. But since I was a young girl, I've been visiting the gravesites of loved ones I've lost through the years.

Listening to my husband's voice was very helpful, too. On the Saturday evening before he died on that Monday, John had videotaped our son's last high school basketball game. We were sitting together in the bleachers and talking while watching. John was always analyzing plays and cheering and supporting Collin and his teammates. Listening from time to time to his voice brought comfort.

Also, various ministries in the church helped me deal with my grieving process. The best thing is always helping others. Eventually, my pastor appointed me as a deaconess, then I later became an ordained deaconess.

Also, family and friends were very supportive throughout my grieving. One of my dear sisters-in-law called me every single day after the funeral to check on me until she felt I was feeling better, doing well, and getting stronger. This helped a lot.

I truly believe grieving has no time limits and varies from person to person, but it can be navigated successfully and needn't take over your life forever.

Fred:

During Carolyn's illness, we discussed what each of us wanted should one pass before the other. My wife, being the unselfish and kind person she was, said she didn't want me to spend a lot of money on her burial and that she wanted to be cremated. Her wish was to have her ashes spread near her favorite casino in Biloxi, Mississippi. A couple of weeks after her homegoing service, my son and I did just that.

We stayed with one of my best friends and his wife. He and I had met in the US Air Force in 1978. His wife, who still calls me by my last name, said, "Kirby, I was upset with you the day of the repass because you seemed happy."

So I explained that I had been solidly grieving with my wife for the last two years. When her health started what we now know was its final decline, I grieved.

When our house burned, I grieved for her grief at the loss of her favorite things, then reminded her that she'd been wanting a new fridge, stove, and floor. But when we went looking for furniture, she picked out all of it and said, "This is your new bachelor furniture." I grieved the loss of a woman who, even as death approached, could make such an unselfish gesture.

When she had to have the tip of a finger amputated because it was dying, I grieved. Each time she had to have a toe amputated, a platelet transfusion, her spleen removed, or cried for more morphine to stop the excruciating pain.

I grieved.

As I watched this most beautiful and energetic life of the party effectively turn into a living mummy as scleroderma hardened and contracted her skin and connective tissue, and doctors would no longer amputate the dead extremities, I grieved.

As he watched his infant son dying, King David didn't eat and mourned. But upon his son's death, he cleaned himself up and sat down to a meal. Folks around him didn't understand. He said, "Now that he has died, why is it I am fasting? Am I able to bring him back again? I am going to him, but, as for him, he will not return to me." (2 Samuel 12:23)

All this, I explained to my friend's wife, is a normal path of grief.

Grief Experiences

Closure

Essay by Ed Gruber

What is this fascination with "closure" as it relates to a death? If it's about a loved one, why close? And what is there to close? The dreadful deed's done; the physical person is gone.

What isn't gone is the pain of the loss. That never gets closed. It lies in the heart and mind in a festering, smoldering mode, too often fired up by a spark of a memory, a random thought, a related incident, a dream, or, more times than not, a nightmare.

The pain of the loss cannot – can never – be willed to close or vanish. This deep dark stinging black hole remains for as long as you live, a steady and ugly reminder of who, what, when, and where. Though never why, the eternal unanswered question. So, what is all this fascination with closure of a pain that truly can never be closed?

Why shouldn't the focus be on certain memories? Those sweet memories that can often be willed to the forefront, or which miraculously — without warning — materialize on their own, blessedly awakened from time to time by a sudden subconscious jolt from who-knows-where, or a real moment in real life, a breeze, a raindrop, a snow crystal, a cloud, a stranger's wave, a train whistle, the blast of an auto's horn, a dog licking your hand, someone who looks like that special someone. Suddenly there is a glorious glint of a time in your history with the deceased that comes alive in your mind's eye and fills the heart with pleasure and warmth. *Take that!* you deep, dark, stinging black hole.

How delicious are these beautiful memories — sweet images of some part of the life and times of the deceased — with the power to induce a smile or evoke a tear that is seldom a grieving tear; a welcomed tear on which a welling tide floats the dearest reminiscences that stir you to whisper, "I am so happy you passed my way. So thankful you were a part of my life. So blessed that I am the person I am because you were in my life."

Closure may have its place in other life experiences. But the death of a loved one? You don't close it. You learn to live with it. You do live with it. And the times when you need a certain lift of spirits and to temper the pain that never goes away, you invite in the sweet memories.

Maybe the concept of closure should be replaced with the notion of acceptance and allowing sweet memories to bring those you love back to life for a brief yet uplifting, passionate, phantom moment. You cannot close the door on the pain of loss of a loved one. But you can open the door and all the windows of your heart and house to those sweetest of memories…and take solace in recollections of the good times.

There is no closure on the death of someone you love. There never should be.

Dedicated to Seth Wayne Gruber (1961-1979) and Shirley Edith Gruber (1929-2013). To my parents, dearest aunts, uncles, cousins, friends, and my U.S. Navy and Marine Corps brothers.

Kieran Pavlick

A widower for 22 years as of this writing, Kieran said, "What is moving on? Twenty-two years later and I have not remarried. And I live alone. I do interesting things like fencing, acting lessons, writing classes. I made a friend. We meet at restaurants and go to events together."

Ed Gruber

"I would not be the man I am today if my wife had not been in my life, so it would be an insult to her not to move on and continue to grow and be the better person she helped create. *Moving on* does not mean forgetting."

Arabella deWilliams

I was not sure if sharing my story of grief would be of use as I have not found a new love. Further, I'm not 100% sure if I am ready for such a thing. However, my heart continually lays the matter at G-DS feet. So, here I go.

My husband realized his dream of retiring before 60 and we moved to Panama, the country, fully intending to live there the rest of our lives. But, after 30 years of marriage, he died unexpectedly. That was seven years ago.

It isn't easy to negotiate the circumstances of death in a foreign country. I look back now and realize my grief had been suspended as my concentration had to go toward tying up loose ends in my newly adopted country in order to move back to my homeland.

For the next couple of years, grief felt like a crushing burden. It wanted to cloud every good thing, and would have if I let it. At first, coping felt rote. I threw myself into helping others. There was no task too large or small for me to turn my attention to with great zeal. But no matter how I spent my time, at the end of the day grief was still ever present.

When I earnestly made the decision to help others out of true heartfelt tenderness and started taking stock of my many blessings, my anguish lessened its hold on me. Sadness now is intermingled with blissful memories.

I've come full circle in my sixties, gathering schoolgirl crushes. My husband and I would sometimes joke about who our celebrity crushes were. I won't go as far to say I love any of my collected crushes but right now they feel like safe havens when I miss romance.

Maybe my story is for that widow not quite sure if they are ready for romance but needs to know it is fine to daydream. My wish for you is shalom. May peace, harmony, wholeness, completeness, prosperity, welfare, and tranquility be yours.

Greg Newland

I do know that each person handles grief differently and it is an individual journey for sure. There are also differences in how men and women process grief and I won't pretend to know anything more than my experience.

Stacey, my wife, and I met briefly in kindergarten, but then a school right by her house was opened during that year and she transferred there. We did not remember meeting in kindergarten. In ninth grade a mutual friend introduced us, but it wasn't until a few years after high school that circumstances brought us together and this time it was real love. We married in May of 1980.

Stacey had Juvenile Type One diabetes. She was diligent in controlling her disease and very healthy when we married. Being married to her, I learned a lot about diabetes. We had some heartache during our first year of marriage. Our son was stillborn at full term.

This was a tremendous heartache for us both, but even more so for her having the child grow inside for nine months and expecting life only to have it not come to be.

Shortly after, the first health issue arose with something called diabetic retinopathy. Laser surgery slowed that down. Like her diabetes, which required regular doctor visits, an ophthalmologist visit also became a regular event. There were some medical things like kidney stones that she seemed prone to which, when it's going on, is pain worse than labor.

We were fortunate to have two daughters. One by the miracle of adoption and one natural but two months premature. The stories about both of those miracles would take too long. Not to generalize, but up until Stacey was 46 she was a fairly healthy diabetic considering that she had it from the age of two.

She had a mammogram and it came back with a questionable area. Because Stacey's mom had died from breast cancer, they decided not to do a lumpectomy but to get aggressive and perform a complete mastectomy. It was sort of a whirlwind for us with no one recommending a second opinion.

She was sent to a surgeon and a plastic surgeon. The plastic surgeon thought Stacey a good candidate for a TRAM (transverse rectus abdominis myocutaneous) flap reconstruction. Basically that means the doctor uses your own body fat and tissue to reconstruct the breast. They call it a TRAM flap because they use your stomach tissue and fat to tunnel it up to the breast area.

Sounds great, right?

Wrong. With long-term diabetes she was not a good candidate for such a thing. Her primary doctor should have stopped it, but didn't. The actual mastectomy was about an hour, the reconstruction another 8-9.

The nightmare was beginning.

She was severely allergic to anesthesia once they started to wake her. For two days she vomited nonstop. Nothing would stop the nausea. Once it settled down we discovered that because of all the vomiting she had ripped what little stomach facia that remained after the TRAM flap.

While there was a slight enticement to this surgery because you get a tummy tuck during the process, after you rip your facia you look like you have the worst hernia ever as organs have nothing to hold them back. (Later they put some mesh in, but it was a mess.)

Also, during the vomiting she strained her head so much she went blind in one eye. Months later they did a vitrectomy which restored the eye's sight, but it was a continuous issue with her sight always declining.

But it was to get worse. She had a stroke which went undiagnosed for a long time due to all the other stuff going on. Once diagnosed, any attempt at rehab was too little too late. Her left side was affected and weaker the rest of her life. I know this is about dealing with grief so I need to fast forward.

As the years went by, she developed severe degenerative back disease. There was some hope that if that could be fixed then she could walk more and get better. Finally, she was able to have a couple of back surgeries, but those only made things worse.

She lived on the couch. No exercise and diabetes is a very bad mix.

To cap it off, she got multiple myeloma (very rare) causing extreme anemia. Weekly blood transfusions followed. Doctors were baffled that the myeloma had progressed so quickly, and so wanted to do a scope of her stomach to see if maybe she had an ulcer or something bleeding causing the anemia. As they were performing the scope they lost her on the table. They went through Herculean efforts to bring her back and put her on life support.

Three days later she passed.

I've left out a lot of details as she had more strokes and a heart attack during her last years. So as you can see, I had a long time to prepare for her passing. She was in a continual downhill slide for 10 years. Now, I had mentioned diabetes her whole life and the doctor who monitored her while on life support told me if they had any idea how bad off she was they would not have resuscitated her. He said she may only be 57 but her insides were 97. She didn't process or digest anything. No wonder she was so sick.

Probably for the last six months of her life I knew she was dying. The exact time I came to understand that only God knows. In any case, I knew and had prepared myself. Since for a long time I had done the cleaning and cooking and shopping and the bills there was no shock to the daily rhythm of life like my father-in-law had when my mother-in-law died. She had done all that stuff and he was lost when she died.

I know many deal with sudden losses. Mine was very different. We both had a deep faith in Jesus. Believe me, I prayed all the time for her. Now, we don't know God's plan or why things happen. We can only put our entreaties into prayers, and hope and trust in Him. That's how I got through the 10 years of her being so ill.

And after she passed, that's how I got through each day. It's how I still get through each day.

For some reason Heaven needed her. I am so looking forward to seeing her and many others as well. We were married 35 years. It's been more than five years since she passed and I miss her everyday. Not to the point of depression, but more wondering what she would think about our grandkids.

I am blessed to have my two daughters, two sons-in-law, and five grandkids, and focus on the blessings, not on what I don't have.

I have dated some but haven't married again. I am open to it but also know, as with all things, it is in God's hands. I should mention that I went to a grief class at my church about a year after she passed. I believe others got a lot more out of the class since it focused on the grief process of dealing with sudden loss, which is much different than my long time preparing and knowing.

My walk with Jesus has given me peace that surpasses all understanding.

Good Grief

Carl S. Jordan

Husband, head of house, leader, bold, invincible, capable of wearing many hats. Suddenly I was thrust into a world of grief bringing fear, doubt, confusion, guilt, frustration — and a broken heart.

My new title? Widower.

In the year 2000 the world had just come through the Y2K scare, and it was an election year. My wife, Jan, and I were active in our community on several levels, enjoying our grandchildren, and were successful. We felt humbled and proud to have reached our goals and we knew that God is good.

Unexpectedly one Saturday morning that year, I found myself following an ambulance carrying my wife. Fighting tears, I begged God to save my Queen. But life would never be the same again.

Jan was admitted into the hospital and diagnosed with pneumonia. The doctors did not like her heart function and suggested we see a heart specialist. She would need a heart transplant. While the doctors were working on that process, she suddenly developed diabetes with precipitous blood sugar drops forcing me into life-and-death fast trips to get her to the ER. Then her thyroid needed to be removed.

Hundreds of doctor visits followed. I don't remember all their names but I can tell you what they did: heart, diabetes, eyes, kidneys, liver, stomach, thyroid, nutritionists, arthritis, and psychologists. In every case I delivered her and waited, waited, waited hours in ER triage, waiting rooms, offices, and pharmacy lines.

Twenty-five pills a day, insulin and, all too often, medications prescribed just to see if they would work. Oftentimes they did not, and time, money, and expectations were exhausted.

Nineteen years we endured this routine. Determination, drive, and faith kept her alive. She continued with her work, though, and the doctors thought that was great because it kept her active and engaged and was great therapy for both of us as we truly enjoyed the work we did repairing hundreds of homes for senior citizens at no cost to them.

Even so, money became an issue and we downsized to reduce debt, reduce monthly expenses, and better prepare for retirement. Through it all, God was good all the time.

At the end of 2015, after three hospital stays that year, the heart doctor said nothing more could be done to improve her condition and we should prepare for the inevitable. We had been told that someone with her condition usually does not last five years. We were in year fifteen by then. After a 16-day ICU stay, the phone rang at home. Jan also had tuberculosis.

Again, action was needed and there was no time to cry. An LVAD (Left Ventricle Assistance Device) was placed in her abdomen with a line coming through the skin to a controller with two batteries. Imagine carrying a small shoulder bag with a brick in it with an attached cord coming out of your stomach that can never be removed or get wet lest you die.

After the LVAD operation, my role of caregiver ramped up with unimaginable responsibilities. Dressing the area around the tube, clothing and bathing, cooking, even sleeping was a challenge.

Through all the stress and turmoil, though, our attitudes kept us grounded, our faith kept us strong, our love kept us committed, and humor lightened the mood.

I thank God for those times because the challenges we were facing and about to face were becoming insurmountable.

The doctors remarked how great our attitudes were throughout these challenges and they were right.

So, I thought that might be a great time to get back to work and even formulated a new company where I could train new agents and work from home. I spent weeks planning and preparing, spending money I did not have, all in an effort to regain some sense of normalcy.

Feb 2, 2017. I woke up in an ambulance. I had passed out from dehydration and my blood pressure was low. OK, I thought, I'll get through this, I have to. I have a wife to take care of. But the doctors found a slow-growing, non-cancerous brain tumor causing hearing loss and balance issues. So it wasn't just me getting old! I figured age might be a factor as I'd never been sixty-eight before.

My brain surgery was scheduled for April 2017. It was the first surgery I had ever had as an adult and hopefully the last. But it wasn't to be. When I woke up from surgery I had double vision. I spent several days in the hospital and could not walk or see, and hearing was now totally different.

I learned through my spiritual awakening that we walk by faith not by sight but when you can't see and can't walk all you have is faith. I prayed a lot but still could not cry. After a year, surgery fixed the eyeball but vision was still not well. It took another year to get approved for stereotactic radiation treatment. Five treatments and still no eye improvement but now I was dizzy and incoherent from swelling on the brain from radiation. Steroid treatment left me feeling like a zombie.

While going through that, my mother died at 90. I still couldn't cry. Three weeks later my wife died. The last words I heard her say were, "I can't take anymore."

God had called her home on our 31st wedding anniversary.

If ever there was a reason to cry this was it. But I was numb. No tears. It was all too much. After a wonderful homegoing, I tried to put the pieces of my life back together but I have continued to struggle with the grief.

I was some place I'd never been before. I didn't know what I didn't know and things I took for granted now seem to be monumental tasks. Once joint decisions are now all mine.

I questioned everything because there was no one to bounce ideas against…and no one to keep me in check and on point.

I carry my loss as evidence of how great things were and can still be! Faith guides me and has brought me through crisis time and again and will continue to do so.

My destination is greater than the crisis.

Joyce Bailey

When I heard about this book being written, I wondered: Am I still grieving?

So I looked up the meaning of grief to find it means deep sorrow. Some synonyms were agony, gloom, heartache, headache, pain, regret, and sorrow. I reviewed my situation.

In July 2016 my husband, Charles, went in for knee surgery. Surgery went great and he came home the next day. Opting to do his rehab at home instead of having to travel to an office for three days, his doctor supplied him with oxycodone and other medicines for pain. Four days in a row everything was going great. On day five, though, he went into congestive heart failure.

EMS was called. He was revived. Then in the ambulance he had to be revived again. At the hospital doctors had to put him on a ventilator. He never came off. One week after his surgery, two days after his heart failing, they pronounced him dead.

I was now a widow with a paralyzed son.

Yes, I was still grieving the unexpected death of my husband. And I'm experiencing grief and pain every day.

But my God is good. He is faithful. He gives my limbs strength to get up every morning. He puts me in a right mind. I give him all the glory. My favorite scripture is Psalm 121 which says in verses 3 and 7:

"He cannot possibly allow your foot to totter. The One guarding you cannot possibly be drowsy…He will guard your soul."

Lisa Ellsworth

I've had several experiences with grief.

Each has been as unique as the relationship I had with each individual. When I was 13, I learned about the passing of my father. This was a man I'd never met because Mother had fled in the night with my sister and me with nothing but the clothes on our backs. I was three months old at that time.

I learned he was violent and unpredictable and my mother feared for her life as well as for my sister and me.

I didn't feel very much emotion for him, but then felt guilty that I did not feel sad. It was very confusing at the time.

Losing my mom was very hard on me. She and I were very close. Even though she was 93 and her passing was expected, it was a horrible shock. In my mind I just thought she'd always be there. I called her every Saturday morning for more than 20 years. I felt a huge void. She was the one I could talk to about anything, and vice versa. I still talk to her and I feel like I know what she would say if she were here. She will live on forever in my heart. I can still hear some of the things she'd always tell me.

"If it's the right thing for everyone, then God will make it happen."

"There is the right solution to every problem, you just need to apply the right thinking."

"Don't make things harder than they need to be."

But the loss of my husband, Blaine, was the hardest. I'm still in a healing process. We were high school sweethearts. He was the only man I ever dated; my one and only true love. We were blessed with 46 years together, have four amazing adult children and nine grandchildren.

With diabetes and kidney failure, his health had been in decline for seven years. Looking back, I must have been in denial about his health. Always thinking he'd get a kidney and be back to himself in no time. (I have been accused of being a Pollyanna!)

Then one day, we were sitting together having a conversation when he took a big gasp of air. Turned out to be his last. All the CPR from me and the medics were not going to save him. He was in God's arms now. A better place without pain or dialysis. For several months I had PTSD about the CPR. I was shocked and felt so hollow. I wasn't ready to be a widow.

Not now. Not ever.

My chaplain told me I had a choice. I could dwell on that last day or I could remember all those wonderful memories of our 46 years together. That helped a lot. I also joined a grief recovery group; talking to others helps. My faith is what pulled me through the most. Knowing that he is with God in a beautiful place, knowing it was only his body that passed away and he will live on in my heart.

Another thing my mom told me when my grandmother passed was "She's only a thought away". It's been just a little over a year and I'm still healing. I feel better and I want Blaine's legacy to live on. I talk about him, reminding our grandchildren how much Papa loves them. I've been blessed that he comes to me in my dreams several times a week.

I will always love him.

V. Harris

The day after Mother's Day, May 11, 2020, was one of the saddest of my life. "Be at the hospital as soon as possible" I was told one morning around nine. I arrived at the hospital a little over an hour later. This was in the middle of the worst of COVID, when we didn't know what was going on with it or where it was going. Extremely strict in-person measures were in place at hospitals, so I had not been able to see or talk with my husband for over a week. Plus, I was only getting minor updates from nurses…when they could be bothered.

I stood by his bedside, told him I loved him. He tried so hard to say he loved me, but he did manage to say "Get me out of here". Then, with all the strength he had left, he pulled the oxygen mask from his face and slipped away. But at that moment I could not cry. I kissed my husband's still-warm arm and hand. For over 30 minutes I simply looked at him, caressing his hands. His face changed as facial muscles begin to relax.

Thinking I could drive home, I walked out of the hospital but got less than a mile away before I had to pull over. The tears were blinding and I sat on the side of the road for a while — I don't know how long. I do not even remember pulling in the driveway at home. I just knew things now had to be done.

I planned the service for that Wednesday. I didn't want to wait a week to have his service. When you only have two days, things happen fast. Wednesday came. Due to COVID only 10 persons could be in attendance. I chose to be the one to put the blanket around him and close the lid on his coffin. I chose to be the one to commit his body. This was my way of showing my darling husband and dear friend that I was still with him until the end.

As I write this, it has been six months and six days since his passing. The first month I cleared out his closet, keeping just a few of his things. His dresser drawers were so neat. He often told me to make mine look neater, sometimes even straightening them for me.

I'm working part time and that helps to fill my days. Our yard was my husband's pride and joy. I've kept it up, cutting grass when I feel up to it or getting lawn help when I don't.

I decided that changes were needed for me to learn to live alone. I've lived as two for forty-two years. I was determined to keep my sanity. We were a couple of faith who believed that everything happens for a reason. We did not and will not question God. We were taught that favor is not fair. God blessed me to still be here. I need to breathe and get on with it.

When I get sad I recognize the moment, cry if I need to, then find something to take my mind off of the past. Things will never be as they were. I remember the good, the bad, the sad, and the indifferent times. I know that I was loved and I pray that I can love again if God has that in his plans for me.

Grief is different for everyone. For me there is some loneliness, but I don't feel alone. This is the first time in years that I have only me to think about.

Change is good. I changed the bedroom color. When it was finished, I cried. We had lived with the same color for 16 years. We used to have competitions making the bed. The most difficult thing to do after he passed was to change it. I put on new bedding. "This looks good, you'd like it," I told him. I still don't sleep on his side of the bed; haven't been able to do that yet.

A fresh, new start even if I may be a little afraid of one, but I am not alone.

Alberta Gray Speakman

In the days, weeks, and months following my husband's death, I swung between mind-numbing grief and an insatiable search for him, for his essence. One moment painfully sad, the next moment I was hunting for his ghost, spirit body, soul — anything that was him. I was overwrought with sadness and lonely for My Lynn. I lost the ability to concentrate and could not read or watch television for the first year. Spending time alone with three doggies, in my private world, thinking, became my preference.

I had no desire to engage in social conversation other than with my family. I could not remember anything negative about my marriage. To me it was perfect. Even though I'd been brought up in it, a religious background didn't help.

In fact, immediately trying to apply my faith to my dire circumstances actually deepened my doubts about what faith really meant to me and life in general, and whether someone I loved dearly was now in a place called heaven, or the afterlife.

The journey that started the day my husband died has been the most important journey of my life. I spent those first few years after his passing barely surviving, and living day in and day out inside a routine that took away passion for life.

A routine based on fear of the future and dictated by my ego's need to protect myself kept me stuck in one place. I hated my life, my future, and every moment of every day.

I was envious of women whose husbands were still alive with their kids out living their perfect lives.

I was a bitter, angry widow.

And the years went by as searching and rote survival continued.

Amazing how the brain likes to loop grief and never let it go. Existing in a never-ending state of grief, waiting for time to heal me, was coupled at the same time with "grief is supposed to last forever".

Those two concepts made me furious because I was spending precious time to waiting to heal.

Looking back, I realize I survived by my instincts. I was always mindful of signals coming from my heart, prompting me how to survive.

No goodbye is forever unless you can erase everything you ever knew about a person and everything you once felt.

Sarah Crossan

After Awhile

by Veronica A. Shoffstall

After a while
you learn the subtle difference
between holding a hand
and chaining a soul.
And you learn that love
doesn't mean leaning
and company doesn't
always mean security
and you begin to learn
that kisses aren't contracts
and presents aren't promises.
And you begin
to accept your defeats
With your head up
and your eyes open
With the grace of woman,
not the grief of a child
And you learn to build
all your roads on today

Because tomorrow's ground
is too uncertain for plans
And futures have a way of
falling down in mid-flight
After a while, you learn that even sunshine
burns if you get too much
So you plant your own garden
and decorate your own soul
Instead of waiting for
someone to bring you flowers.
And you learn that you
really can endure...
That you really are strong.
And you really do have worth.
And you learn and you learn...
With every goodbye,
you learn.

When someone is mourning, there is absolutely nothing you could say to alleviate their pain. Just sit with them, hold their hands, and be present and compassionate.

Anoir Ou-Chad

PART THREE
Moving Forward

Valerie and Fred:

We met through what we believe was a God-guided meeting. On our own, we would never have thought to ask for what the other had and would bring to our lives. But who knows us better than we know ourselves? Who knows what is best for us?

Our Heavenly Father, that's who.

God invites us to be open to what He will provide. Having no preconceived notion of who will work best for us — or even if anyone is necessary — will allow God to provide.

One way of doing this is to examine our grief in detail. There is no right way to grieve and you may find you're doing a fine job of grieving that totally works for you. You should feel good about that. As Elizabeth Kübler-Ross said, there are no "linear timelines of grief".

The Guided Grief Journey [beginning on page 103] will prove helpful.

Relief:

Some people experience relief at the death of a loved one. They could have been in great pain, and their death relieved that pain, so you could also feel that same relief on their behalf. This is normal.

Sex Drive

Stephanie A. Sarkis PhD said that the sex drive may actually increase after a spouse's death. Orgasms release ocytocin (the "bonding" hormone) and endorphins (the "feel good" hormone), which reduces pain perception. The sex drive could also disappear. These are both normal states and can appear in the same person at different times. There is nothing to be ashamed of or to feel guilty about. It is normal to feel these.

Valerie:

I didn't experience a need for sex. My dating was more about the need to be part of a couple as I had been for so long, the having of a companion to go to the movies with or out to dinner, intimacy, and physical touch. I wanted normalcy in my life and being a couple was "normal" for me.

Fred:

It had been nearly two years without any physical closeness or intimacy. I was truly missing it and sought it through online dating sites. But I had to be true to myself. I had to first find out who I was other than "Fred Kirby, Carolyn's Husband".

Grief is so human,
and it hits everyone at one
point or another at least
in their lives.
If you love you will grieve,
and that's just a given.

Kay Redfield Jamison

GUIDED

GRIEF

JOURNEY

Valerie and Fred's answers

Stages of Grief Review

The stages of grief do not come in a set order. We are also not guaranteed they will come swiftly. Sometimes many years will have passed when, out of the blue, you may experience one of these stages. It is not uncommon for those who remain behind to be taken by surprise with the whiff of a scent or the hearing of a sound and immediately be thrust into a cacophony of emotion.

These memories and emotions do not imply that your faith in God is weakened or that you do not love the one you are now with. Far from it! Even God Himself has emotions based on his memories and experiences with others. He's been angry, sad, and has even felt regret. It isn't wrong to feel negative emotions.

Feelings are just that — feelings. They come. They go. Learn from them, but don't let them destroy you.

We will answer each of these questions to show you how different we were in processing the different stages.

When you go through the Guided Grief Journey, your answers can be very different or very alike. There is no right or wrong answer and no one need see what you write. What is most important is to answer your truth about your journey to yourself. Accurate knowledge will serve you well in the long run.

After we answer all these questions, we will provide a section with all the questions again but with plenty of space to write your thoughts in this book, as a handy journal to keep and use as long as you wish.

Stages of grief are:
Denial
Anger
Depression
Bargaining
Acceptance
Moving Forward

Obviously, it isn't the death of your loved one that you are in denial about. But if you are denying something, what is it?

Valerie:

I denied my vulnerability and pretended everything was alright when it wasn't. During our marriage, John had always been the one who handled the pressures. He often joked that because of my strong personality, from the outside people would think I was running things, making things happen for the family, but it was all him.

Fred:

My wife's long-term disabling diseases (scleroderma and Raynaud's) had me denying that it was affecting me at work and so my work suffered.

What is that denial doing to your ability to cope with added pressures in your life? Is that denial hurting relationships and driving others away?

Valerie:

My denial of my own vulnerabilities made me think that I was the one who had to be strong for everybody else. With John gone, everything fell in my lap. I was now both mom and dad. John always led. I followed.

I was told by some of the people I dated that I talked about John too much…just like he was still alive. That turned off some people, but it was part of my grieving. I realize now that I started dating far too soon.

Fred:

I really have had nothing that I've been denying about my life or emotions.

There are no right or wrong answers to any of these questions. If you are not angry, then that's fine. But consider these anyway. Remember you are answering privately to yourself, so be honest. Candor will not harm your heart, it can only heal as you uncover hidden challenges. Even God Himself has righteous anger. So, with whom are you angry? Why?

Valerie:

I was angry with God. I felt he took John away from me too soon. I didn't want to face my new reality of alone. I was scared of the unknown in front of me.

Fred:

I was angry at my late wife's family, specifically her sister and two nieces. They never came to visit except when they needed something. I remember my wife saying, "I wish my nieces would come and do my hair."

With what are you angry? Why?

Valerie:

After John suffered his first heart attack and his doctor released him to start back to work after spending some time in the hospital and recuperating at home, I thought his health was improving. He had been working from home for several months, so it all seemed good.

Fred:

I was angry that the doctors amputated two of her toes and the tip of one finger. I was angry because when her other pinky finger turned black and was dying, we asked if they were going to remove it and they said no, that it would fall off. Why didn't they just let the others fall off, too? My thought was that surgery cost money and we had a tough time with that given the situation.

Are you angry with yourself? Why?

Valerie:

Yes, I was angry with myself. I felt I should have been more in tune with John's health at the time and asked the appropriate questions. Ever since we met as teenagers, he'd been in and out of the hospital and always bounced back. John never complained about how he was feeling. He always displayed a positive attitude about his health. But this time, I felt I should have insisted he not return to work so soon or continue with all of his responsibilities. My thought was, "Maybe he would not have died if only I had…"

Fred:

I am not angry, per se. But I am a little bit disappointed with myself that I didn't feel sad after her passing. I thought that grieving after death meant crying and moping about, but I didn't do that. I came to understand that I had been grieving every day for years as each time she got worse I lost a little bit of her.

But I occasionally feel a little angry with myself simply because I was at work when she went into cardiac arrest. I wasn't there to hold her hand or comfort her. I wish I had taken more time off from work to just talk with and listen to my wife.

Are you angry with your spouse (or other loved one who has passed)? Why?

Valerie:

Yes, I was angry because John did not tell me just how sick he was…at least, I felt like he hadn't. But he had a lifelong illness and I knew about it and knew he was not expected to live as long as he did. I was discouraged from marrying him because everybody said I would quickly be a widow. But he always "beat the odds" and, with his very strong faith, he knew God had a plan for his life.

Fred:

Never could I be angry with her. She endured so much: multiple platelet transfusions, spleen removed, losing toes and tips of fingers, and pain, so much pain.

Are you angry with others? Why?

Valerie:

No, I wasn't. I believe everyone did what they could to be supportive at the time.

Fred:

Other than what I mentioned earlier, no, I was not and am not angry with any others.

Are you angry at the reason you're angry? Why?

Valerie:

I was angry that I felt overwhelmed with all the emotions I was feeling and experiencing. I was angry that I was trying so hard to adjust to my new reality but it was taking longer than I thought it should.

I know it says in Proverbs 13:12 that "Expectation postponed is making the heart sick, but the thing desired is a tree of life when it does come". So I tried to be patient with myself.

Fred:

No.

Depression itself is not one emotional state. It is an umbrella label that can include, among other things, despair, sadness, misery, hopelessness, dejection, and emptiness that usually last awhile and can come and go. Each of those carries its own effect and can vary with each person.

Valerie:

When I went through my depression after losing John, I never had the urge of wanting to bring harm to myself physically or indulge in any type of substance abuse. And I thank God for His faithfulness and protecting me during this season of my life.

I would say that I experienced sadness and a sense of loneliness. I knew God was with me all the time, but I missed John. He was my best friend and soulmate and I loved him very much. We had planned to do so many things together since I had retired, and now I was faced with my new normal.

There were times when I was sad and lonely and withdrew from people and tried to deal with my feelings and emotions alone. I wanted to have personal time to reflect on my own, privately.

My emotions were sometimes raw and I would have emotional outbursts for no reason. Or something would trigger the outburst, like seeing a place we had been to, or hearing a song. Other days I'd be fine and could move on. I'd cry, then snap out of it.

But as time and everyday life moved along, I became stronger and learned how to cope with my emotions. I thank God for His grace and mercy because he never left me. I took time to dig deeper into the Word. That gave me hope to move forward, and moving forward gave me more hope.

Fred:

I did not go through a state of depression.

Death cannot be undone. Still, some people will bargain about it. They want to *make a deal.* If you have done this, with whom are you wanting to bargain? What do you want to accomplish with it?

Valerie:

I never went through the bargaining stage. From long before we were married, I already knew John had health problems. When we married I had already accepted that we wouldn't have long together, and that he could be called home by the Lord at any time.

Fred:

I have had my moments of bargaining — with myself. The "what ifs" worried me some. She was in the Emory Healthcare system and I was thinking that she's getting the absolute best care that can be had. But it doesn't matter who the doctor is, ***you*** have to be your own biggest advocate.

Acceptance: Like depression, acceptance is an umbrella term with much nuance associated with it, such as: to receive, to admit, to consent, to agree to or with, to acknowledge, to endure, and to tolerate. Looking at each nuance and what those look like to you, finish these sentences:

Valerie:

I have received a beautiful granddaughter who is a blessing from God and the joy of my life.

I admit that I am no longer angry with God and I must continue to trust the process of God's Word.

I have consented to moving forward with my life and believing the Word of God and His promises for my life.

I agree to always keep God first in my life and to not look back in such a way that does not allow to have healing.

I agree with the Word of God that He has all the answers.

I acknowledge that John has gone to be with the Lord and that his sweet, loving, and beautiful memories will always have a place in my heart.

I have endured my trials and tribulations. I have gained control over my life.

I have tolerated or am now tolerating the adjustment to my new normal and the reality of life without John.

Fred:

I have received a blessing from God when my grandson was born.

I admit that I was relieved when my wife went to heaven. She suffered tremendously.

I have consented to living my best life.

I agree to carrying on her memories and making sure my grandson knows who his Grandma was.

I agree with God. He makes no mistakes. I was put in Carolyn's life for a reason and a season.

I acknowledge that I was not the perfect husband. I sometimes had to remind myself of that when she got mad. It wasn't about her being mad at me, but it was her pain and her wondering "Why me?"

I have endured: Lots of sleepless days and nights and the pain of seeing my wife suffer for so long. I endured the task of juggling work, supporting my son in school band, and being a caregiver.

I have tolerated or am now tolerating relationships because it was my nature to make others happy.

Are you feeling stuck and can't seem to move on? Why do you want to move on?

Valerie:

I am not stuck. I have moved on with my life. After his first heart attack, John said he did not want me to be alone. I couldn't imagine that ever happening, but he did not want me to be alone.

Fred:

I am not stuck as I started earlier in the moving-on process when, as we were shopping for new furniture after a house fire, Carolyn picked out all the furniture and said, "This is bachelor furniture." Thus she gave me permission to move on with no regrets or guilt having lived up to my vow of 'til death do us part, and gave her the best of care.

Once you've decided what your *moving on* looks like, how will that change your —

Valerie:

Daily routine: Being in my granddaughter's life has brought joy and positive change in my life, for sure. I continued going to the gym, having my morning devotions, lunch with friends and family, enjoying time for self, and being involved in church, professional activities, traveling, and hanging out with my son.

Approach toward others: My approach has gotten more positive and I am enjoying their company and being in their presence.

Outlook at work/church: No change in my outlook with work, which I thoroughly enjoyed, but I am now retired. And I love my church and church family. They have always been supportive.

Self-care: I have stopped putting myself in situations that are only there to make others happy — especially when the others do not truly appreciate my effort.

Fred:

Daily routine: Two days short of my wife's birthday, I had a new grand arrive. But my routine changed. No more did I have to change bandages and dressings. I could come home from work and just sleep. I had worked nights just so I could be with her during the day and available for her doctor appointments. Now I could rest.

Approach toward others: Still steady on. Nothing changed.

Outlook at work/church: At work, I could focus again and that helped with not making mistakes anymore. I also went back to working days instead of nights. Also, I was now able to start back going to church.

Self-care: Resting. Learning to live in a non-emergency state of mind.

I Am Learning How To Live

by Jamey Wysocki

I am learning how to live
In a new way
Since that day
You were taken away.

I am learning how to live
With the things left unsaid
Knowing I got to say them
With every tear that I shed.

I am learning how to live
By embracing the pain
Knowing that you live on
Through the memories that remain.

I am learning how to live
Knowing I will never again see your face
And I have peace knowing
You're in a better place.

I am learning how to live
Knowing you're in God's care
It gives me the strength to move on
And makes the pain much easier to bear.

GUIDED
GRIEF
JOURNEY

Now it is your turn to start your journey through grief.

Stages of Grief Review:

The stages of grief do not come in a set order. We are also not guaranteed they will come swiftly. Sometimes many years will have passed when, out of the blue, you may experience one of these stages. It is not uncommon for those who remain behind to be taken by surprise with the whiff of a scent or the hearing of a sound and immediately be thrust into a cacophony of emotion.

These memories and emotions do not imply that your faith in God is weakened or that you do not love the one you are now with. Far from it! Even God Himself has emotions based on his memories and experiences with others. He's been angry, sad, and has even felt regret. It isn't wrong to feel negative emotions.

Feelings are just that – feelings. They come. They go. Learn from them, but don't let them destroy you.

We answered these questions simply to show you how different we were in processing the different stages. Your answers can be very different or very alike.

There is no right or wrong answer and no one need see what you write. What is most important is to answer your truth about your journey to yourself. Accurate knowledge will only serve you well in the long run.

Stages of grief are:
Denial
Anger
Depression
Bargaining
Acceptance
Moving Forward

Do not feel as if you must rush through these questions. Take them in the order we have them or skip around as is best for you. We have included plenty of space for you to write over a period of time. Your answers may change, so feel free to date your entries to see how your journey has progressed.

Obviously, it isn't the death of your loved one that you are in denial about. But if you are denying something, what is it?

What is that denial doing to your ability to cope with added pressures in your life? Is that denial hurting relationships and driving others away?

There are no right or wrong answers to any of these questions. If you are not angry, then that's fine. But consider these anyway. Remember you are answering privately to yourself, so be honest. Candor will not harm your heart, it can only heal as you uncover hidden challenges. Even God Himself has righteous anger.

With whom are you angry? Why?

With what are you angry? Why?

Are you angry with yourself? Why?

Are you angry with your spouse (or other loved one who has passed)? Why?

Are you angry with others? Why?

Swinton and Kirby

Are you angry at the reason you're angry? Why?

Depression itself is not one emotional state. It is an umbrella label that can include, among other things, despair, sadness, misery, hopelessness, dejection, and emptiness that usually last awhile and can come and go. Each of those carries its own effect and can vary with each person.

Death cannot be undone. Still, some people will bargain about it. They want to *make a deal.* If you have done this, with whom are you wanting to bargain? What do you want to accomplish with it?

Acceptance: Like depression, acceptance is an umbrella term with much nuance associated with it, such as: to receive, to admit, to consent, to agree to or with, to acknowledge, to endure, and to tolerate. Looking at each nuance and what those look like to you. Finish these sentences:

I have received

I admit that

I have consented to

I agree to

I agree with

I acknowledge that

I have endured

I have tolerated or am now tolerating

Once you've decided what your *moving on* looks like, how will that change your –

Daily routine:

Approach toward others:

Outlook at work/church:

Self-care:

Scriptures on Grief to Contemplate

Deuteronomy 31:6-8

Psalm 18:2

Psalm 23

Psalm 30:5

Psalm 55:22

Psalm 121:1-2

Jeremiah 29:11

Matthew 5:4

Matthew 6:34

John 14:1-4

John 14:27

Philippians 4:6

Romans 8:28

BOOKS FRED AND VALERIE FOUND TO BE HELPFUL

When Bad Things Happen To Good People
— Harold S. Kushner

Conversations with God
— Neale Donald Walsch / a 10-book series

The Power of Being Thankful — Joyce Meyer

A Grace Disguised — Jerry Sittser

You Can Begin Again — Joyce Meyer

Closer To God Each Day — Joyce Meyer

Healing After Loss
— Martha Whitmore Hickman

Finding Humor in Grief
— Dr. Ruth L. Baskerville

The Year of Magical Thinking
— Joan Didion

RESOURCES

National Suicide Prevention Lifeline
(800) 273-8255

WhatsYourGrief.com
Eleanor Haley, M.S.
Program Director and Co-Founder
eleanor@whatsyourgrief.com

Litsa Williams, M.A.
litsa@whatsyourgrief.com

speakinggrief.org

For various losses: **grieving.com**
Best live chat: **griefincommon.com**
Facebook groups list: **griefanonymous.com**
Groups: onlinegriefsupport.com/groups
Email groups: **griefnet.org**
Monitored discussion:
griefhealingdiscussiongroups.com

Search on Facebook and Instagram for groups dealing with grief.

Finding purpose, accepting what cannot be changed, instead of always saying "Why me?"

Video: The Art of Saying Goodbye
Isabel Stenzel Byrnes at TEDx Stanford
www.youtube.com/watch?v=Dkffpibi-Dc

Visit our website to connect with us on Social Media.

ACKNOWLEDGEMENTS

We would like to thank **God** for giving us the vision to write this book.

To our parents (rest in heavenly peace), **Love and Doris Collins, and Fred and Rebecca Kirby**, we thank you for bringing us into this world and laying a strong foundation early on in our lives. It's because of your unconditional love is who we are today.

To our courageous sons, **Fred J. Kirby, III** and **Collin J. Swinton**, keep pursuing your goals, dreams and excelling in life. We are so proud of you both!

To our precious grandchildren, **Levi G. Kirby and Chloe N. Swinton**, you know we love you! You are the joy of our life!

To our family and friends, thank you for your support.

We are grateful to our spiritual father, Bishop Gary Hawkins, Sr., for your leadership, guidance, and powerful teaching of Gods word.

This book was written to all that have encountered loss of a loved one. Our desire is that the stories shared in this book will give you hope in new beginnings.

ABOUT THE AUTHORS

Valerie D. Swinton is an ordained deaconess at Voices of Faith Ministries in Stone Mountain, Georgia. She is a retired elementary school principal who provided 31 years of service in public education serving as an elementary teacher, special education teacher, school counselor, assistant principal for instruction, and elementary principal.

She holds a Bachelor of Arts degree in Child Development and a minor in Early Childhood Education from Spelman College, a Master of Arts degree in Special Education and a minor in Learning Disabilities from Clark Atlanta University, and a Specialist in Education degree with a focus on Administration and Supervision from Georgia State University. She is a member of Delta Sigma Theta Sorority, Incorporated.

In 2004, she was honored by the Georgia Department of Education for making the list of Outstanding Achievement Schools. The list honored the top thirty schools from across Georgia that had significantly increased student performance on state assessments. In 2007, Valerie received the Honorary Life Membership award presented by the Parent Teacher Association in Georgia from her students, parents, teachers, and the community for outstanding service to children and youth. In addition, she has been a national presenter and trainer at various educational conferences throughout her career.

Fred J. Kirby exemplifies an abundance of business acumen and service as a licensed Real Estate Broker for 30 years. His journey began when he enlisted in the United States Air Force after his high school graduation. While in the military, he attended leadership school and Noncommissioned Officer Training. He strengthened his entrepreneurial skills by joining Century 21 Real Estate as a salesperson.

Later, Fred launched his own company, Kirby Realty Services, which has assisted many first-time buyers to their delight with home ownership.

Fred's unique quality to help others resonates among friends, families, and even strangers. He cherishes relationships and loves to create lasting and lifetime memories. As an avid traveler, he enjoys new adventures and the wonderful experiences of creative, tasty cuisines.

Was this book useful to you?
If yes, then please
recommend it to others
and write a review on Amazon.com.

Would you like the authors to come speak to your group? Please visit their website at www.softtouchpublishing.com and send them a message. They will get in touch with you.

GOOD GRIEF
VALERIE D. SWINTON
FRED J. KIRBY

SOFT TOUCH PUBLISHING
SNELLVILLE, GEORGIA